This is the true story of Destiny,
a brave little sloth who did not let an
injured eye keep her from learning
how to be free in the rainforest.

NATIONAL GEOGRAPHIC
WASHINGTON, D.C.

squirrel
monkey

The tropical rainforest of Costa Rica
echoed with music from colorful birds,
the *eee, eee, eee* of darting squirrel monkeys,
boom, boom, boom from howler monkeys,
chirps and clicks of cicadas, and a whispering
rustle from the wandering breeze
in green treetops.

toucan

howler
monkey

5

Down on the ground there was the soft *ah, ah*
of a frightened baby sloth who had fallen
and could not climb back up to find her mother.
She heard the *cree, cree* of a poison dart frog
and the *ssssss* of a deadly bushmaster snake.

The little sloth was hungry, weak, and sick,
with thin hair, itchy skin, and a sore eye.

Her cries might have attracted cats called ocelots
or stray dogs, if she hadn't been found by people
who were kind enough to call an expert—
a scientist who knew how to rescue sloths,
nurse them back to health, and return them
to the forest.

At an animal rescue center, the little sloth was given medicine and goat's milk.

The scientist took her home at night, so she could be fed every few hours. All rescued sloths deserve names, so the scientist decided to call this one Destiny, a word that sounds strong and free.

At first, Destiny seemed too weak to recover completely, and the scientist wasn't sure she would ever be safe in the wild.

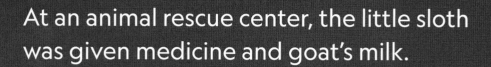

8

Grogu, another sloth at the rescue center, drinks goat's milk.

9

Destiny munches on guarumo leaves.

Destiny's sore eye did not heal.
She could not see well, and she often
lost her balance.

Fortunately, Destiny loved to eat,
and the food helped her grow.

The scientist put Destiny in a small basket
draped with floppy green guarumo leaves
and bright pink hibiscus flowers,
wild foods that Destiny's mother
would have taught her to choose
if they were clinging to each other
high in the treetops.

Eating made Destiny strong, and curiosity kept her moving, so she never gave up trying to learn how to climb, even when poor eyesight made her fall.

Destiny and Fiona (left)

12

Destiny and
Dory (right)

Best of all, Destiny was friendly.
In the wild, adult sloths live alone,
but in the rescue center, Destiny
loved to hug other orphans,
comforting them and showing them
how to eat, as if she was
their teacher!

13

When it's time to poop, three-fingered sloths hold on to the base of a tree ...

With an appetite, confidence,
and friends,
Destiny graduated from the
rescue center's
sloth preschool.

The next step was to learn to survive
outside the safety of the
rescue center's walls.
First lesson—potty breaks!

She was carried outdoors,
where the scientist set her down
on the ground in soft, wet leaf litter
at the base of a small tree.

... and wiggle their little tails to dig a hole to bury their waste in. It's called the poop dance!

Then, Destiny lifted her head to gaze upward,
reached with long arms and curved fingers,
clasped the smooth trunk of the little tree,
and started climbing!

She paused and listened
to the scientist's encouraging voice.
There were so many other sounds
in the forest, toucans cracking palm nuts,
macaws squawking,
and the squeaks and shrieks
of capuchin monkeys
as they leaped from tree to tree
like acrobats.

macaws

Smells were fascinating, too.
Hot, moist air rich with savory leaves
and fragrant flowers.
The stink of a tamandua
and the stench of a porcupine.
With only one healthy eye,
Destiny sniffed all sorts of scents
as she studied her surroundings,
moving slowly
and carefully
from one tree
to another
without
falling.

tamandua

Destiny held on to each new branch
with three of her four shaggy limbs
before letting go of the last branch.
Cautiously, she peered with her one eye
in every direction, to make sure she was safe
as she gradually mastered
the most important sloth skills—
finding food
and hiding from predators.

With her one eye, she spotted a floating blue morpho butterfly and a shimmering, iridescent hummingbird.

blue morpho butterfly

When she was relaxed and happy, Destiny scratched her hair, huddled in the rain, then dried off in the sun and enjoyed the cool movement of a refreshing wind.

Destiny relaxes in the treetops.

21

Branches swayed, but Destiny
kept her balance.

Each day at the center,
she grew stronger
while she practiced new skills.

When a year had passed,
the scientist weighed Destiny and
decided that she had reached the size
when her mother would have known
she was ready to feed herself
and be independent.

She was finally big enough to be released.

Destiny is
weighed during
a checkup.

To prepare Destiny for the wild,
the scientist fitted a tracking collar
around her neck, so that she could be
monitored to make sure
she was safe.

Destiny was taken to a release cage
that was left out in the forest,
with an open door
so that she could leave
whenever she was ready.

It's time for Destiny to go out into the forest on her own.

The little sloth was brave!
She did not hesitate.
With her one good eye
she looked all around,
surveyed her surroundings,
and then—confident and curious—
she ventured
out of the cage,
reached
to grab
a tree trunk,
and climbed
up
up
up toward
wild
natural
freedom!

A note from the author

The text for this book was inspired by wildlife conservationist Sam Trull's photographs of Destiny, and by stories she shared while I was visiting the Sloth Institute in February 2020. By then, Destiny had been released in the rainforest and was living freely. But I had the chance to meet other orphans, as well as adult sloths rescued after they were injured by electrical lines or other hazards. It was not my first trip to Costa Rica, but it was my first close encounter with a scientist like Sam, so dedicated that she took baby sloths home at night so she could wake up and feed them every few hours.

Li'l Sebastian, one of the other sloth orphans, has also been released now, but he was three months old at the time of my visit. He lived in a basket in the rescue center, cuddling his pink blanket, drinking goat's milk, and munching on floppy *Cecropia* leaves. He was a student in Sam's "sloth preschool." She took him out-doors and gave him a chance to dig a hole with his stubby tail, poop, and then climb a small tree. He kept looking back at her, checking to make sure his substi-tute mommy was watching. I was surprised by his intelligence, sweet personality, and resilience. Sam told me something I will never forget: She said sloths at the rescue center are friendly to each other, and loving to humans, as if they understand that they are being helped.

The assistant director of the Sloth Institute, Pedro Felipe Montero Castro, led me on a walking tour of the rainforest, pointing out sloths and other animals hid-den in the canopy above us. Pedro also said something I will never forget: *"Todo el mundo sabe rescatar, pero nadie sabe liberar*—Everyone knows how to rescue, but no one knows how to release." He and Sam explained that they receive frequent calls from people who have found orphaned or injured sloths, rescued them, and don't know what to do next. A scientific approach like the one at the Sloth Institute is needed. Rescued animals need to be healthy and educated—prepared for independence—by the time they're released.

I was surprised to learn that diurnal three-fingered sloths like Destiny and Li'l Sebastian have a life span of 20 years, while the nocturnal two-fingered species can live more than 40 years. That's a long time to keep a sloth in captivity, so the goal of release is essential, not only to maintain the wild population, but for each individual sloth's happiness. Even though sloths can't really smile (see page 31), they are happy up in the trees, resting, eating, scratching, climbing, and looking around at their surroundings. They're not lazy, just careful. Unlike monkeys that leap, sloths never let go of one branch until they're already clinging to the next branch. I left the Sloth Institute knowing that I had learned a lot about life, as well as quite a bit about sloths. I learned from the slow perseverance of sloths, and from the dedication of scientists who prepare them to enjoy lifelong freedom.

—Margarita Engle

A note from the photographer

Almost every day for the past decade I have taken at least one photo of a sloth—usually a lot more than one. As the co-founder and executive director of the Sloth Institute in Costa Rica, I am very often surrounded by sloths and find myself unable to resist the temptation to press that shutter button. Sloths sleeping, sloths climbing, sloths going to the toilet; no matter what they do I am there, camera (or phone) in hand, and ready to document it. In addition to photographing sloths, I am also one of the main people providing their daily care. Feedings and medical treatments are frequent occurrences for our sloth patients that are being rehabilitated for a life back in the wild.

Thanks to our work at the Sloth Institute, we have rescued almost 400 sloths in Costa Rica. Sadly, that number only increases over time as sloths struggle to deal with human encroachment. They are often injured by electrocution when they touch uninsulated electric wires that run through their forest homes, or get attacked by dogs (who have no home themselves) when they descend to the ground to cross canopy gaps. Many of our patients come to us as orphans when their moms are killed in one of these horrible accidents or when forest loss has displaced them to make room for new buildings or to improve the view of the ocean from every hotel floor.

Some of our rescues are with us for only a day, some a few months, and others (the orphans) can stay in rehabilitation for up to two years! Destiny was one such orphan. Rescued at only a couple of months old, she was found after she had fallen from her mother, sick and with only one working eye. We arrived on the scene with our veterinarian, and while we always try to reunite mom and baby sloths when possible, it was clear that if we didn't rescue little Destiny, she was going to die. Her mother, who was in a tree above us, was ignoring Destiny's cries for help, which is unusual for mother sloths. Usually they find a way to the ground or wherever the helpless baby may be and

retrieve their precious cargo. However, at close inspection we could see that mama sloth already had another baby on her chest ... Destiny was a twin! There isn't a lot of research about sloth twins because usually sloth moms have only one baby at a time. However, raising a baby uses a lot of energy. Because sloths need to conserve energy to survive, raising two babies at one time would be quite difficult—especially in a fragmented forest with changing or inadequate food resources.

Luckily for Destiny, we were nearby and able to step in and not only save her life, with the help of our friends from Toucan Rescue Ranch, but also eventually return her to the wild. Despite having only one eye, she never stopped fighting—and we never stopped fighting for her. Every day, sloths struggle with how to coexist in an ever changing, fast-paced environment. Saving sloths like Destiny is an integral part of how we can right the wrongs that wildlife face and conserve wild populations of sloths.

—Sam Trull

29

This map shows where Destiny was rescued in Costa Rica and other places three-fingered sloths live in North America and South America.

NORTH AMERICA

MEXICO

GUATEMALA

HONDURAS

Caribbean Sea

EL SALVADOR

NICARAGUA

COSTA RICA

PANAMA

The Sloth Institute
Where Destiny
was rescued

VENEZUELA

French
Guiana
(France)

ATLANTIC OCEAN

COLOMBIA

SURINAME

GUYANA

ECUADOR

PACIFIC OCEAN

BRAZIL

SOUTH AMERICA

PERU

BOLIVIA

PARAGUAY

Where three-fingered
sloths live

0   500 miles

0   500 kilometers

ARGENTINA

ATLANTIC OCEAN

Arctic Ocean

NORTH AMERICA

Atlantic Ocean

EUROPE

ASIA

Pacific Ocean

AFRICA

Pacific Ocean

SOUTH AMERICA

Indian Ocean

AUSTRALIA

Southern Ocean

ANTARCTICA

30

Want to learn more about sloths?

ABOUT THE SLOTH INSTITUTE

The Sloth Institute (TSI) is a nonprofit organization located in Costa Rica with the mission to enhance and expand the welfare and conservation of sloths through rescue, rehabilitation, release, research, and education. In addition, TSI works on targeted conservation projects to improve the safety and quality of sloth habitats and teaches other rescue centers how to better care for and release their sloths. TSI believes that all sloths were born to be wild and deserve that second chance at freedom.

theslothinstitute.org

BOOKS

Swing, Sloth! Explore the Rain Forest, by Susan Neuman

Sharks vs. Sloths, by Julie Beer

A Little Book of Sloth, by Lucy Cooke

WATCH

The episode "Monster & Africa" from the TV series *Nature's Miracle Orphans* (PBS)

Facts About Sloths

There are two main types of sloths—two-fingered sloths and three-fingered sloths. One way you can tell the difference is by the number of fingers they have on their hands. Destiny is a three-fingered sloth.

- Three-fingered sloths look like they're always smiling, but that's an illusion. Sloths don't have the muscles they would need to make different facial expressions, but the coloring on their faces helps give them their smiley look.

- Three-fingered sloths have more bones in their necks than giraffes do.

- Sloth hair has nooks and grooves in each strand that collect water. Algae grows in those grooves and helps the sloths blend in with their green tropical forest habitat and avoid predators.

- Being slow helps sloths save energy, carefully climb through the rainforest, and be quiet so predators can't hear them.

- Sloths are losing their habitat as people cut down trees for buildings and roads.

- Conservationists are building rope bridges (also called sloth speedways) to help sloths cross areas where trees have been cut down, so they can reach other parts of their habitat.

three-fingered sloth

two-fingered sloth

31

For future wildlife rescue superheroes —M.E.

Published by National Geographic Partners, LLC.

Text copyright © 2023 Margarita Engle
Compilation copyright © 2023 National Geographic Partners, LLC

Since 1888, the National Geographic Society has funded more than 14,000 research, conservation, education, and storytelling projects around the world. National Geographic Partners distributes a portion of the funds it receives from your purchase to National Geographic Society to support programs including the conservation of animals and their habitats. To learn more, visit natgeo.com/info.

For more information, visit nationalgeographic.com,
call 1-877-873-6846, or write to the following address:

National Geographic Partners, LLC
1145 17th Street NW
Washington, DC 20036-4688 U.S.A.

For librarians and teachers: nationalgeographic.com/books/
librarians-and-educators

More for kids from National Geographic: natgeokids.com

National Geographic Kids magazine inspires children to explore their world with fun yet educational articles on animals, science, nature, and more. Using fresh storytelling and amazing photography, *Nat Geo Kids* shows kids ages 6 to 14 the fascinating truth about the world—and why they should care. **natgeo.com/subscribe**

For rights or permissions inquiries, please contact National Geographic Books Subsidiary Rights: bookrights@natgeo.com

Hardcover ISBN: 978-1-4263-7234-6
Reinforced library binding ISBN: 978-1-4263-7235-3

Printed in China
22/PPS/1

I thank God for wild animals and the scientists who help them. I'm grateful to my family and friends, Sam Trull, the Sloth Institute, Pedro Felipe Montero Castro, Tulemar, and Dave Houck. Special thanks to my agent Michelle Humphrey, editor Angela Modany, and the whole publishing team. —Margarita Engle

Thank you to our friends at Toucan Rescue Ranch, especially Leslie Howle, for taking care of Destiny in the first few months of her life before our rehabilitation facilities were built. I always enjoyed my visits to bring her fresh leaves and help with her nightly feedings. Thanks to our vet Janet, who is not only a wonderful friend but also the world's best sloth vet. Thanks to Tulemar, especially Dave Houck, for giving TSI a home and always believing in our mission. Thanks to my husband and TSI assistant director, Pedro Montero, for staying up late at night to help me feed babies like Destiny and for everything you do to help me keep TSI running. Last but not least, thank you to Tom Lawrence and all of the TSI volunteers who stay out day and night tracking sloths like Destiny after they have returned to the wild so that we can be sure they are living their best sloth life. —Sam Trull

The publisher would like to thank everyone who worked to make this book come together: Angela Modany, editor; Lori Epstein, photo manager; Julide Dengel and Sanjida Rashid, designers; Mike McNey, map production; Alix Inchausti, senior production editor; and Anne LeongSon and Gus Tello, associate designers.

Author photo on back flap & p. 28, Shevaun Williams; blue morpho butterfly on p. 21, Hannamariah/Shutterstock; watercolor texture, Jenny Solomon/Shutterstock; plant pattern, Eteri Davinski/Shutterstock. All other photos by Sam Trull.